A TRUE BOOK™

T0011444

DIGGING IN GEOLOGY

All About Fossils

Discovering Dinosaurs and Other Clues to the Past

Cody Crane

Children's Press®
An Imprint of Scholastic Inc.

Content Consultants

Dr. Thomas R. Holtz, Jr.
Principal Lecturer in Vertebrate
Paleontology, Department of Geology,
University of Maryland, College Park

Dr. Wen-lu Zhu
Professor of Geology
Department of Geology
University of Maryland, College Park

Library of Congress Cataloging-in-Publication Data
Names: Crane, Cody, author.
Title: All about fossils : discovering dinosaurs and other clues to the past / Cody Crane.
Other titles: All about fossils
Description: New York : Children's Press, an imprint of Scholastic Inc, 2021. | Series: A true book | Includes
    index. | Audience: Ages 8-10. | Audience: Grades 4-6. | Summary: "This book introduces readers to fossils"—
    Provided by publisher.
Identifiers: LCCN 2020035264 | ISBN 9780531137161 (paperback) | ISBN 9780531137123 (library binding)
Subjects: LCSH: Fossils—Juvenile literature. | Paleontology—Juvenile literature.
Classification: LCC QE714.5 .C73 2021 | DDC 560—dc23
LC record available at https://lccn.loc.gov/2020035264

Design by Kathleen Petelinsek
Editorial development by Priyanka Lamichhane

Scholastic Inc., 557 Broadway, New York, NY 10012

4 5 6 7 8 9 10 R 30 29 28 27 26 25 24 23 22

Front cover: Many different types of fossils are found all over the world. Fossils can tell us a lot about what life on Earth was like long ago, from ancient insects to mighty dinosaurs.

Back cover: The fossil of Dippy the *Diplodocus* is made up of 292 individual bones. The bones were first discovered in 1898 by railroad workers in Wyoming.

Find the Truth!

Everything you are about to read is true *except* for one of the sentences on this page.

Which one is **TRUE**?

T or F Fossilized poop can reveal what prehistoric creatures ate.

T or F Fossils show that life first appeared on Earth 8 billion years ago.

Find the answers in this book.

What's in This Book?

The **BIG** Truth

Are Dinosaurs and Birds Related?

Archaeopteryx

A fly trapped in fossilized tree resin called amber

Paleontologists work to uncover fossils at the Mammoth Site in South Dakota.

5

Dig In!

Fearsome **saber-toothed cats**, massive **mammoths**, and the powerful *Tyrannosaurus rex* once roamed Earth. But these creatures are now **extinct**. No more of their kind can be found on Earth. **So how do we know they ever existed?** Because they left behind **fossils**. Fossils are the preserved remains or traces of ancient lifeforms. All sorts of living things, from land animals and plants to insects and sea creatures, can form fossils. It is the job of scientists called **paleontologists** to study fossils so we can learn more about the history of life on Earth.

Tyrannosaurus rex was both huge and powerful. It grew as long as 40 feet (12 meters) and had jaws strong enough to crush a car.

Saber-toothed cat

Trilobite fossil

Complete dinosaur skeletons are rarely found. The versions in most museums are copies of real fossils.

Dippy the *Diplodocus* was one of the first dinosaur skeletons to ever go on display, in the early 1900s. Replicas of the fossil have been shown in different museums, including this one at a museum in Glasgow, Scotland, in the United Kingdom.

Pieces of the Past

Dinosaur bones are some of the BIGGEST fossils around. But bones aren't the only types of fossils paleontologists find. Ancient creatures can leave behind all sorts of evidence that they existed, from nests to footprints. These fossils form in different ways, and they provide clues as to what life was like long, long ago. Let's take a look at different types of fossils and how they are created.

Colorful minerals make up this piece of fossilized wood from Arizona's Petrified Forest National Park.

The word "petrify" means to turn into stone.

Petrified Fossils

After a plant or animal dies, its soft tissues usually decay. Leaves, skin, or muscles rot away. Hard body parts, such as beaks or bones or a tree's wooden trunk are also left behind. But under certain conditions, these parts can become **petrified**. This means minerals fill in the spaces in the hard parts, and sometimes even replace the original tissues. What remains are fossils of the body parts of the animal or plant, which have hardened into rock. Most dinosaur fossils are petrified.

How Bones Turn into Stone

Here's how the hard body parts of a dinosaur's skeleton, such as bones, teeth, and claws, can turn into petrified fossils.

1 A dinosaur died near water where **sediment**, such as sand or mud, covered its body. Its soft tissues, such as skin and organs, rotted away. A layer of sediment protected the remaining skeleton from decaying.

2 More layers of sediment piled on top of the animal's remains. As groundwater slowly dissolved material that made up the animal's bones, minerals in the water seeped into tiny, microscopic holes in the animal's skeleton.

3 The layers of sediment above pressed down on those below, squeezing them until they turned to rock. Over millions of years, the slow movement of **tectonic plates** pushed the layer containing the fossil up to the surface.

4 After many more years, wind and water wore away rock on Earth's surface. This revealed a bit of the fossil. It is then up to paleontologists to find the remains and dig them up!

Mold and Cast Fossils

Mold fossils are impressions, or outlines, of once-living things left behind in rock. Sometimes a plant or animal dies and falls into sediment. Then the mud or sand hardens around the creature, and its body decays. What remains is a hollow space shaped like the original plant or animal. If minerals fill this mold fossil, they can harden into a cast. A cast fossil looks like an exact copy of the original organism.

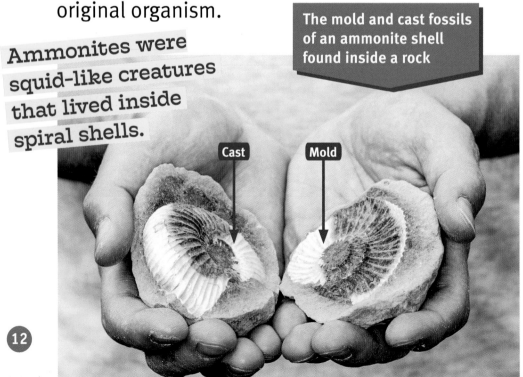

Ammonites were squid-like creatures that lived inside spiral shells.

The mold and cast fossils of an ammonite shell found inside a rock

Cast

Mold

Dinosaur footprint

Dinosaur eggs in a nest

A piece of fossilized poop is called a coprolite.

Fossil turtle poop

Trace fossils can reveal what animals ate, where they traveled, and how they reproduced.

Trace Fossils

Footprints or a trail left in mud by a dinosaur dragging its tail are examples of trace fossils. Preserved nests, eggshells, underground burrows, and fossilized poop are trace fossils too. Like other fossils, trace fossils form through petrification, or when an impression left in sediment hardens into rock. These fossils can tell scientists how ancient animals behaved.

Trapped!

Millions of years ago, a bug landed on the branch of an ancient pine tree and became stuck. Pine trees ooze resin. Small animals, such as insects, can get trapped in this sticky liquid. Over time, the resin can harden into **amber**, fossilized tree resin, preserving the animal's body inside. Large ancient animals, such as mammoths and saber-toothed cats, became trapped in tar in a similar way. Tar is a gooey, oily substance that seeps up from underground. It can preserve an animal's bones without changing them into stone.

Scientists have found this prehistoric fly, as well as other insects, lizards, snakes, and frogs, trapped in amber.

Frozen in Time

It is so cold in parts of Russia that the ground is frozen year-round. The icy environment has preserved the bodies of many animals for tens of thousands of years. In 2007, a Russian man stumbled upon one of the most fascinating frozen fossils ever discovered. It was the body of a baby woolly mammoth. Scientists named her Lyuba (LOO-bah). Because she was frozen, her skin, trunk, fur, and even her organs had been almost perfectly preserved.

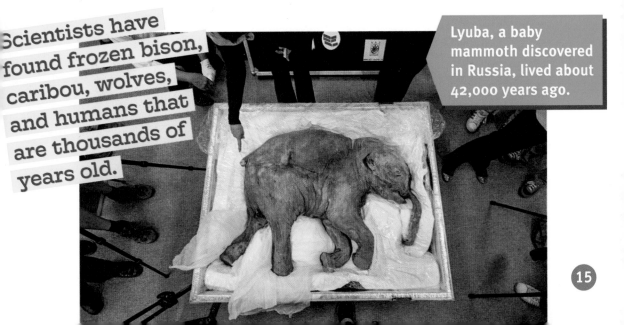

Scientists have found frozen bison, caribou, wolves, and humans that are thousands of years old.

Lyuba, a baby mammoth discovered in Russia, lived about 42,000 years ago.

Marine animals were some of the very first creatures living on Earth. The first fish appeared almost 500 million years ago.

Earth's land once formed a single large continent, called Pangaea, surrounded by a vast ocean.

A Record of Earth's History

Earth has gone through many changes during its 4.5-billion-year history. Mountains have risen, seas have dried up, and continents have shifted. Paleontologists know a lot about our planet's past thanks to the fossil record—the history of life on Earth told by fossils. The fossil record reveals the variety of plants and animals that thrived during different periods. This provides hints as to what Earth's climate and landscape were like in the past.

Keeping Track of Time

Scientists have divided Earth's past into four major units of time called eras. Eras are divided into smaller units of time called periods. Each of these divisions is marked by a big event that affected the planet. These events included major changes to the climate, the appearance of many new lifeforms, or catastrophes that caused huge numbers of creatures to die. Scientists learn about these events by studying fossils created before and after each event.

Timeline of the Evolution of Life on Earth

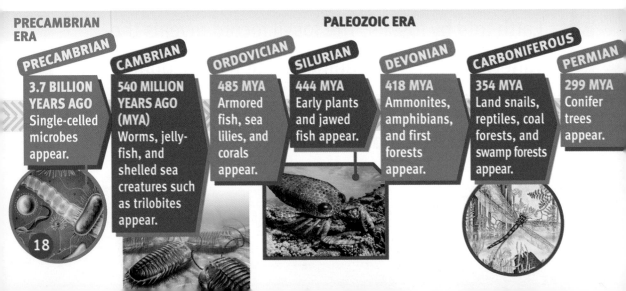

PRECAMBRIAN ERA

PALEOZOIC ERA

PRECAMBRIAN
3.7 BILLION YEARS AGO
Single-celled microbes appear.

CAMBRIAN
540 MILLION YEARS AGO (MYA)
Worms, jellyfish, and shelled sea creatures such as trilobites appear.

ORDOVICIAN
485 MYA
Armored fish, sea lilies, and corals appear.

SILURIAN
444 MYA
Early plants and jawed fish appear.

DEVONIAN
418 MYA
Ammonites, amphibians, and first forests appear.

CARBONIFEROUS
354 MYA
Land snails, reptiles, coal forests, and swamp forests appear.

PERMIAN
299 MYA
Conifer trees appear.

Bursting with Life

No life existed on Earth for more than one billion years after our planet formed. Then about 3.7 billion years ago, tiny single-celled **microbes** appeared. From there, fish and corals appeared, followed by early plants and amphibians. Then forests began to grow. Next came reptiles, birds, and finally mammals. Today, there are millions of **species** on Earth. But millions more have existed and gone extinct during our planet's long history.

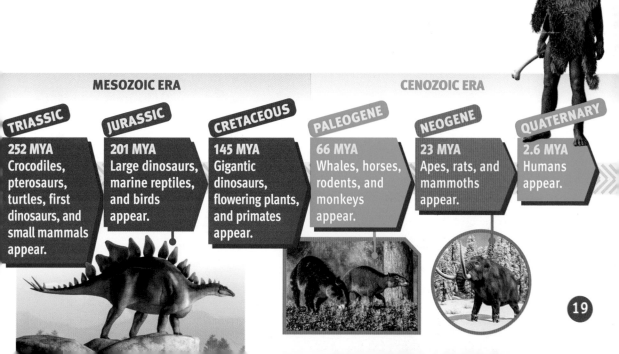

MESOZOIC ERA

CENOZOIC ERA

TRIASSIC

252 MYA
Crocodiles, pterosaurs, turtles, first dinosaurs, and small mammals appear.

JURASSIC

201 MYA
Large dinosaurs, marine reptiles, and birds appear.

CRETACEOUS

145 MYA
Gigantic dinosaurs, flowering plants, and primates appear.

PALEOGENE

66 MYA
Whales, horses, rodents, and monkeys appear.

NEOGENE

23 MYA
Apes, rats, and mammoths appear.

QUATERNARY

2.6 MYA
Humans appear.

Wiped Out!

There have been five mass extinctions in Earth's history. During each one, changes in plant life, increased volcanic activity, or other environmental changes may have altered Earth's atmosphere, which caused temperatures to drastically cool or warm. Many creatures could not survive and became extinct. The last mass extinction occurred during the time of dinosaurs. Scientists believe a huge space rock crashed into Earth, blocking out the sun. Earth became too cold for the dinosaurs, and they died out. This marked the end of the Mesozoic Era.

Scientists think a dino-destroying asteroid left a 93-mile-wide (150-kilometer) crater in what is now the Yucatán region of Mexico.

Dinosaurs went extinct about 66 million years ago.

Woolly mammoths were covered in thick hair. This kept them warm, helping mammoths survive in their freezing habitat.

Ice Ages

Periods of time when Earth's climate greatly cooled are known as **ice ages**. They have occurred five times in the planet's past. During an ice age, freezing temperatures caused the ice caps at Earth's poles to spread, covering as much as one-third of the planet in ice. The most recent ice age ended about 11,700 years ago, during the current Quaternary period. Early humans roamed Earth and hunted woolly mammoths for food.

Are Dinosaurs and Birds Related?

Many paleontologists do not think dinosaurs completely went extinct. Instead, they believe dinosaurs began evolving into birds about 150 million years ago. When dinosaurs went extinct, those that had already started this change survived. Scientists have discovered fossils with both dinosaur- and birdlike features that have helped them piece together how this change may have happened.

2 Some dinosaurs, including *Compsognathus* (komp-SOGH-nay-thus), developed feathers that covered their bodies.

1 Over time, dinosaurs that walked on two legs became smaller and smaller.

22

4 The evolution continued and modern birds appeared. They had developed beaks and gained the ability to fly. Most paleontologists consider them living dinosaurs!

3 Dinosaurs continued to gain birdlike features. *Archaeopteryx* (ar-kee-OP-turr-icks), one of the first true birds, had wings but dinosaur-like teeth, tail, and claws.

Archaeopteryx fossil

Fossils have been found on every continent, even Antarctica.

The Mammoth Site in South Dakota has the greatest number of mammoth fossils in the world.

CHAPTER

3

Fossil Hunters

Being a paleontologist is like searching for buried treasure. Instead of looking for gold, these scientists search for fossils! How do paleontologists know where to find them? They visit areas with **sedimentary rock**. One of the places this rock formed was near prehistoric rivers, where layers of mud and sand piled up. Creatures that died near a river sometimes got buried in its sediment. This gave them a good chance of being preserved within sedimentary rock as fossils.

Detective Work

When fossil hunting, paleontologists carefully scan an area. They look for anything interesting lying on or sticking out of the rocks. They often explore hillsides where wind and water have worn away rock, exposing fossils. Fossils often look just like regular rocks. But paleontologists know to watch out for certain patterns, textures, and shapes. They may spot the swirl of a fossilized shell or bones that are a darker color than the surrounding rock.

Fossil shells like these are often found among rocks along England's Jurassic Coast.

Fossil Hot Spots

Fossil beds can be found all over the world. These sites contain many well-preserved fossils, usually from a particular period of time. The map below shows some of the most well-known fossil beds and examples of the fossils found there.

Location: Hell Creek, Montana, and North and South Dakota
Fossils: *T. rex* and other Cretaceous dinosaurs

Location: Jurassic Coast, England, United Kingdom
Fossils: Sea creatures, from ammonites to giant reptiles

Location: Siberia, Russia
Fossils: Ice age woolly mammoths

Location: Liaoning, China
Fossils: Feathered dinosaurs and birds

Location: La Brea Tar Pits, California
Fossils: Ice age mammals such as mammoths and saber-toothed cats

Location: Plaza Huincul, Argentina
Fossils: Giant dinosaurs such as *Titanosaurus*

Location: Malapa, South Africa
Fossils: Early humans

Location: Antarctic Peninsula
Fossils: Fossil forests

Location: Ediacara Hills, Australia
Fossils: Precambrian soft-bodied animals that resembled worms or jellyfish

NORTH AMERICA

EUROPE

ASIA

AFRICA

SOUTH AMERICA

AUSTRALIA

ANTARCTICA

Tools of the Trade

Once paleontologists find a fossil, it's time to **excavate**. First they dig and carefully expose the fossil. To do this, paleontologists use small tools. The goal is to remove a fossil from the surrounding rock without damaging the fossil. The fossil is then wrapped in cloth strips that have been dipped in sticky plaster. The coating will harden and protect the fossil while it is moved to the scientists' lab. Check out a paleontologist's tools of the trade.

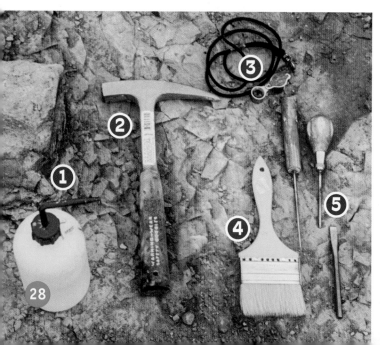

1. **Special glue:** Applied to fossils that are cracked or crumbling to hold them together
2. **Rock hammer:** Used to gently chip away at rock surrounding a fossil
3. **Magnifying glass:** Allows paleontologists to take a closer look at a fossil's features
4. **Brush:** Helps sweep aside debris so paleontologists can see what is underneath
5. **Picks and chisels:** Used to carefully break away and remove rock around fossils

A titanosaur's thighbone is taller than an adult human.

Workers reconstruct one of the most complete titanosaur fossils ever found. The entire skeleton stands two stories tall and stretches 122 feet (37 meters) long.

Puzzle Pieces

Back at the lab, fossils are cataloged. Scientists number each fossil and record where and when it was found. Next, they try to identify what species the fossil belongs to. Scientists put fossils that are broken or have separate parts back together. Most of the time, though, fossils are not complete. This can make it hard to learn what a creature looked like. It's like trying to solve a jigsaw puzzle with pieces missing!

This *T. rex* is named Sue after Sue Hendrickson, the woman who discovered it. It is on display at the Field Museum in Chicago, Illinois.

A *T. rex* skeleton contains about 380 bones!

CHAPTER 4

Amazing Fossil Finds

In 1990, a group of paleontologists were fossil hunting in South Dakota. Sue Hendrickson, a member of the team, spied some giant bones sticking out of the ground. It turned out the fossils belonged to the most complete *T. rex* ever uncovered! The skeleton has helped scientists learn a lot about this species, from how it moved to how big it grew. It is one of the greatest fossil discoveries ever made. Here are some other amazing fossil finds.

When it was alive, this nodosaur was 18 feet (5.5 m) long and weighed almost 3,000 pounds (1,361 kilograms).

This nodosaur's fossil skin had traces of red pigment, which provided a clue to its color.

Beyond Bones

In 2011, a worker found something unusual in a mine in Alberta, Canada. While drilling through the rock, he uncovered a nodosaur (NO-doh-sore) fossil. This fossil not only had a skeleton, but it still had bony plates, spikes, and scaly skin. Scientists think a flooded river carried the dinosaur's body out to sea. There, it sank and was rapidly buried in sediment. The fast rate at which the dinosaur was covered preserved body parts.

Fossil Folklore

People have been finding fossils for thousands of years. But they didn't always know what the objects were. It was once thought that giant bones, horns, and teeth belonged to mythical creatures.

FOSSIL		MYTHICAL CREATURE

Ancient rhino

An ancient one-horned creature related to modern-day rhinos lived until about 39,000 years ago. It could have been the source behind the legend of unicorns.

Unicorn

Megalodon's tooth

Sharks have been on Earth longer than dinosaurs, so it is common to find their fossilized teeth. The largest ancient shark, the megalodon, was longer than a school bus. During the 15th and 16th centuries, people believed megalodons' teeth and other sharks' teeth were hardened dragon tongues.

Dragon tongue

Ancient elephant's skull

Ancient elephant skulls may have inspired the Greek myth of a one-eyed giant called a cyclops. The center of each skull seems to have a single eyehole. It is actually where the elephant's trunk attached.

Cyclops

Battle Scene

In 2009, paleontologists found some fossils that showed two ancient animals locked in battle. A pterosaur (TER-uh-sor), a type of flying reptile, must have been soaring over an ocean. Then, SNAP! A large fish leaped from the water and latched on to the pterosaur's wing. Tangled together, the pair crashed into the water and died in the struggle. Their bodies sank and were buried together in sediment, leaving behind this amazing fossil.

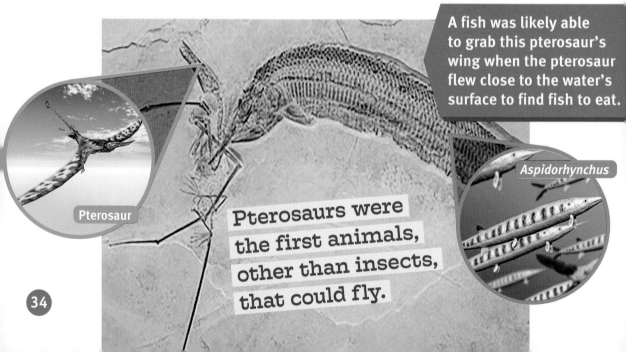

A fish was likely able to grab this pterosaur's wing when the pterosaur flew close to the water's surface to find fish to eat.

Aspidorhynchus

Pterosaur

Pterosaurs were the first animals, other than insects, that could fly.

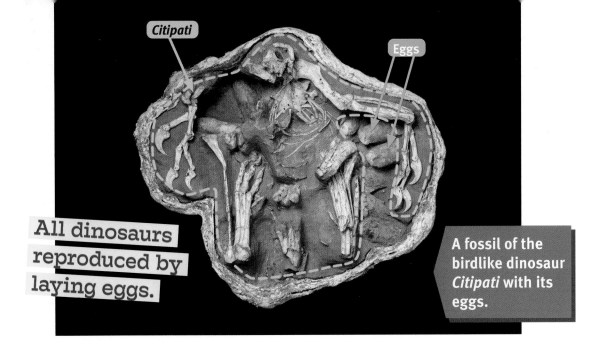

Citipati

Eggs

All dinosaurs reproduced by laying eggs.

A fossil of the birdlike dinosaur *Citipati* with its eggs.

Loving Mama?

Scientists are still trying to figure out if dinosaurs cared for their young in nests. A fossil of the dinosaur *Citipati* (SIT-i-puh-tih) has helped scientists learn more about this mystery. Paleontologists in Mongolia discovered a fossil of *Citipati* in a nest. Its arms were covering eggs, likely protecting the babies and keeping them warm. This was good evidence that some dinosaurs did in fact nest to protect their young.

Scientists estimate there are about 500 coelacanths remaining in the Indian Ocean.

Coelacanths are rarely seen or caught because they live in deep waters.

Living Fossil

In 1938, a scientist was sent a picture of an unknown fish caught in South Africa. He thought it looked a lot like a coelacanth (SEE-lah-kanth). But the coelacanth was thought to have gone extinct 66 million years ago. The scientist later saw the fish in person. It was a coelacanth! This fish has become the most famous example of a living fossil—creatures that have not **evolved** much and still closely resemble their fossil ancestors.

Meet Some Fossil Scientists

Discover how four real-life paleontologists improved our knowledge of ancient life on Earth.

MARY ANNING was born in England in 1799. When she was 12, she found the first ichthyosaur (IK-thee-uh-sor). She later found another huge marine reptile, the first plesiosaur (PLEE-see-uh-sor). Anning's work was well-respected, even though she lived in a time when people thought women could not be scientists.

LOUIS PURNELL fought in World War II with the Tuskegee Airmen, a group of African American pilots. He then worked at the National Museum of Natural History and traveled the world's oceans writing about marine life and studying paleontology. His writings are still used today.

KAREN CHIN is a leading expert on coprolites, or poop fossils. She hunts for these fossils and examines them in her lab. Coprolites can contain bits of plants, bones, or shells that reveal what prehistoric creatures ate. And this helps Chin learn what the environment was like where they lived.

JACK HORNER discovered the first dinosaur eggs in North America. He also found evidence that dinosaurs cared for their young and nested in groups. Horner inspired the paleontologist character in the movie *Jurassic Park*.

Anyone can become a paleontologist. If you were to study fossils when you grow up, what kinds of ancient lifeforms would you want to discover?

11 Fantastic Fossil Facts!

1

The word "fossil" comes from the Latin word *fossilis*. It means "dug up."

2

Fossils have been found on every continent on Earth.

3

Fossil shells have been found on top of Mount Everest, revealing that its rocks once lay beneath an ocean.

8

If you identify a new type of fossil plant or animal, you get to name it!

7

X-rays of fossil dinosaur eggs have revealed babies that had been developing inside.

6

The largest dinosaur fossil footprint is as long as an adult human.

6 FEET

5 Preserved remains need to be at least 10,000 years old to be considered a fossil.

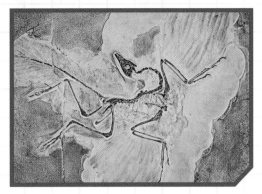

4 The word "dinosaur" comes from Greek words that mean "terrible lizard."

The most common fossils are those of underwater creatures with hard shells.

9 David Shiffler was the youngest person to ever find a fossil. When he was three years old, he discovered a piece of a dinosaur eggshell.

10

11 The oldest fossils are stromatolites. These mounds are the remains of large numbers of microbes that grew together.

Dating Fossils

Scientists can learn how old fossils are by looking at the rocks around them. This is because sedimentary rock builds up in layers over time. Fossils found in lower layers are older than those in layers above. Study this diagram showing fossils within rock layers and then answer the questions that follow.

Analyze It!

1 Which layer of sedimentary rock is the oldest? Which layer is the youngest?

2 Which fossils are older, those of ferns or bony fish? How do you know?

3 Which layer shows two animals that lived around the same time?

4 Why do you think that some fossils that are found in older layers are not found in newer layers? Explain your reasoning.

Fossils within Rock Layers

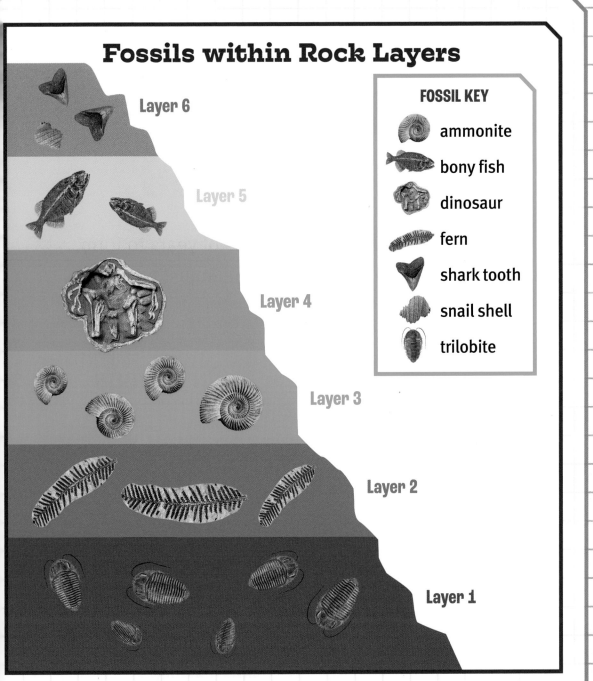

Layer 6

Layer 5

Layer 4

Layer 3

Layer 2

Layer 1

FOSSIL KEY

ammonite

bony fish

dinosaur

fern

shark tooth

snail shell

trilobite

Make Your Own Fossils

Fossils take thousands to millions of years to form. But you can make your own at home in just a few days.

Materials

1 cup flour
½ cup salt
¼ cup water
Large bowl
Spoon
Large plate
Plastic dinosaurs or other toy animals
Seashells
Plant leaves

Directions

1 In a bowl, mix the flour, salt, and water until the ingredients form a dough.

 2 Scoop up the dough mixture and set it onto the plate. Use your hand to flatten out the dough.

3 Press the feet of a toy animal into the dough to make a trail of footprints. Try making imprints of other objects, like toy animals' bodies, seashells, and leaves.

4 Allow the dough to dry for two to three days. It will harden, preserving the impressions.

Explain It!

Using what you learned in the book, explain how the experiment is similar to how some fossils form. If you need help, turn back to page 12.

True Statistics

The length of the largest *T. rex* fossil ever discovered: 42 feet (13 m)

The length of the largest fossil shark tooth, which belonged to the gigantic megalodon: 7.4 inches (18.8 cm)

The age of the oldest fossils, which show evidence of ancient microbes: 3.7 billion years

The weight of *Argentinosaurus* (ar-jen-tin-oh-SOR-us), the largest dinosaur ever discovered: 110,000 to 220,000 pounds (50,000 to 100,000 kg)

The width of the largest ammonite shell ever found: 6 feet (2 m)

The number of dinosaur species that have been named: More than 1,000

Length of the longest petrified tree: 237 feet (72 m)

Did you find the truth?

(T) Fossilized poop can reveal what prehistoric creatures ate.

(F) Fossils show that life first appeared on Earth 8 billion years ago.

Resources

Other books in this series:

 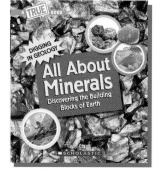 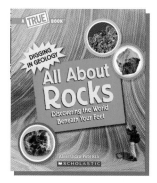

You can also look at:

Brown, Cynthia Light, and Grace Brown. *Explore Fossils!* White River Junction, VT: Nomad Press, 2016.

Pellant, Chris. *Discover Science: Rocks and Fossils*. New York: Kingfisher, 2014.

Waters, Kate. *Curious About Fossils*. New York: Grosset & Dunlap, 2016.

Glossary

amber (AM-bur): a yellowish-brown substance formed from fossilized tree resin

evolved (i-VAHLVED): when living things changed slowly over time

excavate (EK-skuh-vate): to dig in the earth to search for something buried

extinct (ik-STINGKT): no longer living

fossils (FAH-suhls): the preserved remains or traces of once-living things

ice ages (ise AY-jez): periods of time when ice covers a large part of Earth

microbes (MYE-krobes): microscopic, single-celled creatures

paleontologist (pay-lee-uhn-TAH-luh-jist): a scientist who studies fossils

petrified (PET-ruh-fide): when minerals seep into the remains of living things turning them into fossils

sediment (SED-uh-ment): material that settles at the bottom of a liquid

sedimentary rock (sed-uh-MEN-tur-ee rahk): rock that is formed from layers of sediment that have been pressed together

species (SPEE-sheez): a group of living things that all share common characteristics

tectonic plates (teck-TAH-nik playts): giant, slow-moving rock slabs that make up Earth's surface

Index

Page numbers in **bold** indicate illustrations.

About the Author

Cody Crane is an award-winning children's writer, specializing in nonfiction. She studied science and environmental reporting at New York University. Before becoming an author, she was set on being a scientist. She later discovered that writing about science could be just as fun as doing the real thing. She lives in Houston, Texas, with her husband and son.